Christianity at Work

A scriptural study guide for
SMALL BUSINESS
Big Heart
How One Family Redefined
the Bottom Line

Paul Wesslund and Sue Mink

Christianity at Work

A scriptural study guide for
SMALL BUSINESS
Big Heart
How One Family Redefined the Bottom Line

Paul Wesslund and Sue Mink

Heart Ally
Books, LLC

Christianity at Work
A scriptural study guide for SMALL BUSINESS, BIG HEART: How one family redefined the bottom line

Cover photo by Christopher Fryer

Copyright ©2022 Paul Wesslund and Sue Mink
All rights reserved, including the right to reproduce this book or portions thereof in any form whatsoever.

Scripture taken from the Common English Bible®, CEB® Copyright © 2010, 2011 by Common English Bible.™ Used by permission. All rights reserved worldwide. The "CEB" and "Common English Bible" trademarks are registered in the United States Patent and Trademark Office by Common English Bible. Use of either trademark requires the permission of Common English Bible.

Published by:
Heart Ally Books LLC
26910 92nd Ave NW C5-406, Stanwood, WA 98292
Published on Camano Island, WA, USA
www.heartallybooks.com

ISBN-13: 978-1-63107-045-7 (paperback)
ISBN-13: 978-1-63107-046-4 (epub)

1 2 3 4 5 6 7 8 9 10

For Jane, who brought us together

Contents

Bringing the Bible back to earth—a guide to the study guide 1

Chapter 1: What does the Lord require?—Can I really do justice, love mercy, and walk humbly in today's world? 5

Chapter 2: Making a place at the table—feeding body and soul... 17

Chapter 3: When community calls—listening to God 31

Chapter 4: It's not "just business"—the bottom-line case for faithful integrity... 41

Chapter 5: When the going gets tough—going through life instead of around it 57

Chapter 6: Bringing yourself to the table— Christian accountability in the workplace 69

About the authors... 81

Also by Paul Wesslund 85

Bringing the Bible back to earth
—a guide to the study guide

Two true stories.

After discussing the story of the rich young ruler (Mark 10:17–22), a man in a Bible study class I was leading asked, "So do I have to sell my house and live under a bridge in order to follow Jesus's teachings?"

—Sue Mink

I'm reading the news in my local coffee shop when a man enters, stands in the doorway, and declares, "Jesus died for your sins," and walks back outside. I put down my reading. I didn't doubt the man's sincerity, but I had to wonder, as an act of evangelism, was that a good thing, a harmless and neutral thing, or a bad thing?

—Paul Wesslund

Jesus and the Bible seem to set the bar pretty high for us. Sometimes it seems impossibly high. At worst, following its lessons seems so far out of reach it gives us an excuse to give up, to tell ourselves it's not relevant to everyday life. Maybe more commonly we just get discouraged.

That doesn't have to be.

Small Business, Big Heart tells the story of restaurant-owning couple Sal and Cindy Rubino, who spent much of their lives living out scriptural lessons in business and a sometimes difficult family life. But the most inspirational and instructive part of that story comes in how they developed a management style based on compassion.

They actually started out straying from their college dreams of a friendly little café. They sought to strike it rich by building a chain of restaurants until that business crashed, nearly taking their family down with it. They reinvented themselves with a goal of family first, coincidentally about the same time they got involved with a church community that opened their eyes to a more active Christian faith. Then, desperate to find workers for their new restaurant, they somewhat skeptically opened themselves up to considering hiring refugees and people in substance abuse recovery.

That second-chance hiring turned into a business philosophy that would shape the rest of their lives, and even lead directly to financial success. They didn't see their actions as guided by God until they reflected on them much later. When they finally sold the restaurant as a deliberate part of their retirement planning, they could feel they made a difference in the industry, passing it to new ownership by showing that decency, spirituality, and business do go together.

Sal and Cindy offer a real-life story of how scripture succeeds even in the brutal restaurant business: how the same code applies in church, at home, and at work.

Sal and Cindy's guiding principles were as basically Christian as treating others like you'd want to be treated, and giving people second chances. They're old lessons that are more relevant than ever today, as too often we lead by judging each other, reacting with anger, and generally watching out mainly for ourselves. The business model Sal and Cindy created offers bottom-line solutions for a post-pandemic world where a "great resignation" has people seeking more humane working conditions. It speaks to the compassion required to address even world crises as big as substance abuse and refugees.

Sal and Cindy's example shows that decency is not just good, it leads to success. Their example also offers hope for us by adding a dose of relevant reality. Their story is a difficult one, as many of ours are, but one that ultimately leads to showing "how one family redefined the bottom line."

This study guide matches scripture with Sal and Cindy's life and asks questions that apply their story to all of us so that we can realistically live as Christians.

Chapter 1:
What does the Lord require?
—Can I really do justice, love mercy, and walk humbly in today's world?

The Café in Louisville, Kentucky, isn't fancy. Housed in a former manufacturing building by a railroad trestle, it's bright and airy, but almost stark in its simplicity. The menu is full of familiar, homey foods like Reubens, grilled cheese, and tuna melts. The workers are busy but offer warm smiles as they greet their customers, many of them regulars. It immediately feels genuine, without pretension. It's exactly as it appears to be.

    Its founders, Sal and Cindy Rubino, wanted it that way. In fact, that's the way they strive to live their lives. Authenticity is deeply important to both of them. As Sal and Cindy built up the restaurant, hired and trained its staff, and attracted customers, they also began to adopt the ethics and values that they had been learning as growing Christians and putting them into practice in their business. As their business became more successful, they learned how to honor Christ on a daily basis by actually living out Jesus's teachings about compassion, justice, and mercy. They took chances on people by hiring refugees and recovering addicts. They made their family and their employees' families a priority. Their faith touched every aspect of their lives and became the foundation of their business, not just platitudes on Sunday morning.

That authenticity was especially important in their relationships with their employees. Cindy said, "I wanted them to see that we were who we said we were."

That might be more accurately paraphrased as "We *needed* them to see we were who we said we were." The Café couldn't offer the best benefits or pay, so to keep valued employees it needed the best working conditions. It was a business philosophy that came from Sal's teenage years riding with his father in his work truck, listening to him talk about the value of honesty and decency on the job. It came from Cindy's resolve not to treat employees the way she'd been treated in the cutthroat restaurant business. And it came from what might seem like surprising lessons from a church community: even high Christian ideals have a place on the positive side of a balance sheet.

But Sal and Cindy would be the first to say it's a struggle.

Our culture often divorces Christian ethics from business practice, using competitive pressures as

Mark 10:17-22

¹⁷ As Jesus continued down the road, a man ran up, knelt before him, and asked, "Good Teacher, what must I do to obtain eternal life?"

¹⁸ Jesus replied, "Why do you call me good? No one is good except the one God. ¹⁹ You know the commandments: Don't commit murder. Don't commit adultery. Don't steal. Don't give false testimony. Don't cheat. Honor your father and mother."

²⁰ "Teacher," he responded. "I've kept all of these things since I was a boy."

²¹ Jesus looked at him carefully and loved him. He said, "You are lacking one thing. Go, sell what you own, and give the money to the poor. Then you will have treasure in heaven. And come, follow me." ²² But the man was dismayed at this statement and went away, saddened, because he had many possessions.

an excuse to ignore compassion and kindness. How many times do people say "It's just business" when making professional decisions? The demands of Christianity seem much too extreme to apply to the business world. How can we succeed financially if we set our priority on Christlike behavior?

In the story of the rich young ruler (Mark 10:17–22, also Matthew 19:16–22, Luke 18:18–23) Jesus told a young man eager to follow him that he must give up everything he had in order to gain eternal life. Defeated, the man turned away. It's understandable. How could you actually leave everything behind to follow Christ? How can we balance the demands of responsibility to ourselves and our family with the radical demands of Jesus Christ?

The usual response is to soften the demands of Jesus. After all, Jesus knows that we need to take care of ourselves. Surely Jesus is human enough to know the challenges of running a business or even paying the bills. It doesn't seem reasonable to expect us to change our lives that radically. We look for loopholes. We search for reasons why we don't really have to obey.

Perhaps the biggest loophole we find is in defining grace. After all, isn't grace the forgiveness of sins? Jesus died so that we can be forgiven. We're all sinners, and we'll never be perfect, so the best we can do is muddle through and then just ask for forgiveness.

We've been taught that Jesus is just waiting for us to repent and make everything okay.

But that means that grace does all the work and that we can just remain unchanged, our lives untouched by Christ.

In reality, grace is an invitation to be a beloved child of God and to follow Jesus, and by accepting grace, we accept the new life that Christ offers. That is a life of discipleship, of obedience, and of the challenging work of rejecting the shortcuts and devoting ourselves to recognizing and living by the demands of Christ.

At one point Sal sought one of those shortcuts by asking Cindy for a divorce. He saw his life as a mess. His business failed. Earning income seemed to require long hours, and then the demands of being a husband and father took more energy and hours than there were in the day. He wanted out, wanted to change the game. He rented an apartment and prepared to reinvent himself as a bachelor. When Cindy refused his request for a divorce, he got a glimpse of how you have to work through, not around life—a lesson it would take him years to fully learn.

When Jesus delivered the Sermon on the Mount, he ended by telling his listeners that those who followed his words would be wise, like a man who built his house on a rock (Matt 7:24–25). There was no room for personal interpretation, picking and

Matthew 7:24-25

[24] "Everybody who hears these words of mine and puts them into practice is like a wise builder who built a house on bedrock. [25] The rain fell, the floods came, and the winds blew and beat against the house. It didn't fall because it was built on bedrock."

choosing what applied to each of them, or discussing it as an ideal. The command was to go out and do it.

This tension between God's call and the pressures of the world has been evident since the time God first created human beings and gave them free will. Over and over again, even God's chosen people, the Hebrews, slipped away from devotion to God and into a place of rote ceremony that just checked their spiritual boxes. But that was never what God wanted. When the Hebrew people asked God if they should sacrifice more calves, rams, and oil, and even offer their children in sacrifice in order to please God, God responded by asking not for the sacrifice, but for a change of heart and life:

> *And what does the Lord require of you?*
> *To act justly and to love mercy*
> *And to walk humbly with your God.*
> (Micah 6:8)

The Hebrew word in this verse for acting justly is *mispat,* which is a verb. Acting justly is a responsibility and characteristic of ethical living, not just something to talk about or wish would happen. *Mispat* isn't just treating your neighbors fairly, although that's certainly part of it. It's to be aware of exploitation and inequality and to make decisions that promote justice. *Mispat* is outward looking. It's not demanding justice for yourself but, instead, making sure that others have the rights and opportunities that they deserve.

Cindy wanted her own business to be a place of *mispat*, offering opportunity and justice, though she phrased it differently. "I always said if I had a place where I could run my kitchen I would run it fair and honest and treat people with dignity," she said. At one point she took a dilemma to a church retreat after hearing reports of conflicts on her days off. One refugee who worked in the kitchen didn't seem to be involved in the conflicts, but she had little restaurant experience and spoke almost no English; maybe Cindy could give her more responsibility despite her lack of traditional qualifications. At the retreat, Cindy asked whether she should take a chance on promoting someone who had less experience, but who did have values that more closely matched hers. The answer came back a clear "yes," and the result was an employee who stayed more than 15 years.

"Loving mercy" in the Micah verse is sometimes translated as "loving kindness" or "embracing faithful love." All of those are translations of the magnificent Hebrew word *hesed*, which is usually used to describe God's everlasting, never-ending, and all-encompassing love for us and for creation. But *hesed* isn't just a blessing to us from God. God asks that we mirror the love to others that God showers on us. It means seeing the value in others beyond what they can do for us. It means giving second chances. It means making spaces for those who might not seem worth the effort.

At first Sal didn't consider it worth the effort to hire people in treatment for substance abuse. Actually, he didn't think much about it at all until a persuasive counselor suggested it. Like many of us, Sal had preconceived doubts about "those kind of people," but he was desperate for workers. The first hire worked out pretty much as he expected, staying a short time as a dishwasher. The second would shape The Café's business model. Coming from a loving family and a good school, he exploded Sal's stereotypes of a drug user.

"He was the All-American boy next door," said Sal. "It totally changed my perspective. These people aren't necessarily homeless derelicts…. They could be your friend's kid…. It wiped away that whole stigma."

Overcoming that stigma would, over the years, teach The Café two important lessons about seeing the value in others. One is about giving a person a second chance, the other about giving a whole group of people a second chance. Having an employee in a treatment program might require tough love. Relapses do happen, and any employee needs to be held accountable for getting their work done and keeping the business going. If they don't show up, they may have to be fired. But as one treatment center employee who worked with Sal points out, that doesn't mean you give up on the whole group of people. He said, "Don't let the actions of a few rob you of the opportunity to reap the benefits of an employee in true recovery."

In the end, hiring people in treatment both helped give individuals second chances and gave The Café good and long-term workers.

"Walking humbly with God" means that God is your constant companion. The word used for "humbly" here might be better translated as "carefully" or with wise judgment. God asks us to put God's will first, allowing God to guide and direct our decisions.

One of Sal and Cindy's most important insights came from Cindy's father, who said, "Seek the truth and you shall be set free." They didn't know it then, but it was a paraphrase of John 8:32. The exact quotation is "If you hold to my teaching, you are really my disciples. Then you will know the truth and the truth will set you free." Walking humbly with God is holding on to God's teachings and using them as life's plumb line. It's living your life by the truth of Christ.

It can be rare to find people like Cindy and Sal who are actually confronting the challenges of authentic Christianity and making real changes to their lives. But Sal is careful to say that their business decisions were not necessarily made on the basis of their faith. They were what seemed right to them at the time, and, looking back, they now see that they had been guided by God all along. Later, as they came to understand authentic Christianity, Sal saw his faith as something he lives, rather than something he talks about. "We're just trying to do our work and doing it in a way that honors him."

Sal and Cindy each grew up in Christian families. But as adults, they re-entered their faith, not so much through scripture, but through everyday life encounters. A neighbor invited Cindy to an Easter service and then dinner afterwards. A Sunday school class rallied around new church members when their son was injured. Cindy especially was surprised to be accepted by a church family that knew nothing about her. It was a way of accepting and lifting up other people that Sal and Cindy would understand only when they looked back on it—they would find themselves walking humbly, then later realize they were walking with God.

Sal and Cindy's example shows that you don't have to sell all your possessions and live under a bridge in order to walk humbly with God. They didn't. But what they did was to examine the roadblocks in their lives that were keeping them from doing what they knew God wanted them to do. Then they rearranged their priorities to align them with God's. And it changed their lives.

Questions:

1. What tensions have you felt in your life between living a life of authentic Christianity and trying to make it in the world? What choices have you made that have impacted either your spiritual life or your career?

2. What excuses do people make to lessen the demands of Christ? How does the misunderstanding of grace impact authentic Christianity?

3. How are you meeting the demands of Micah 6:8? What are you doing well and where can you improve?

4. Do you try to let God guide your actions, or do you realize later you were being guided? Does it make a difference?

Chapter 2:
Making a place at the table
—feeding body and soul

Food unites people. When friends get together, they often meet for a meal. Families catch up on their day over dinner. Holidays are usually celebrated around a table. Eating together is communal, binding people together in an intimate, shared experience.

Because sharing a meal is a social as well as a personal experience, Jesus was often criticized for eating with people who others felt were inappropriate. If he really was a man of God, he wouldn't be eating with sinners! Yet, that is exactly what he did. Jesus knew that table fellowship is uniquely suited for people to make connections and that sharing a meal enabled him to bond with those who needed to hear his message of love and acceptance. Eating together creates a slower, calmer space to be heard.

Perhaps that is why Cindy and Sal's Café was such a comfortable place for those who were struggling and needed an accepting community. In Louisville, where The Café is located, the pastor of

Crescent Hill Baptist Church understood how many of his congregants who were immigrants and refugees felt about The Café.

He said, "When you're in the restaurant business, you're in the spiritual business whether you recognize it or not. You're satiating the stomach's desire but also the desire for connection with other people, and a connection with something that goes unseen."

The connection between food and community is a theme of Sal and Cindy's lives that developed for both of them from growing up in households that made a point of gathering for family dinner. When Cindy first experimented with a recipe, she shared the soup she made with the housekeeper, turning a set of ingredients into a communal experience. Sal and Cindy even met in restaurant school. The relationships they formed with refugee employees led to invitations to share home-cooked meals with traditions and cuisines from cultures all over the world.

Our traditions as Christians revolve around table fellowship. One of our most important sacraments is that of communion, a re-enactment of the last meal that Jesus had with his disciples before his crucifixion. Communion literally means "sharing." It's much more than eating something together. It's the fellowship of believers reaffirming their commitment to one another and to God.

1 Corinthians 11:17-22

[17] Now I don't praise you as I give the following instruction because when you meet together, it does more harm than good. [18] First of all, when you meet together as a church, I hear that there are divisions among you, and I partly believe it. [19] It's necessary that there are groups among you, to make it clear who is genuine. [20] So when you get together in one place, it isn't to eat the Lord's meal. [21] Each of you goes ahead and eats a private meal. One person goes hungry while another is drunk. [22] Don't you have houses to eat and drink in? Or do you look down on God's churches and humiliate those who have nothing? What can I say to you? Will I praise you? No, I don't praise you in this.

In the early church, when congregations would gather to celebrate communion, or the Lord's Supper, they would also eat a full dinner together with the purpose of sharing their faith as they shared their food. But many early congregations found the table fellowship of the Lord's Supper to be challenging because of economic differences in the congregation. The meals turned into events that were about eating rather than a community honoring the Lord. Paul reprimanded the Corinthian church because more wealthy congregants would eat first, consuming the best foods without waiting for those detained by work or other duties (1 Cor. 11:17–22). The poor, who were those who really needed the food, were left out of the celebration. The entire point of joining together in faith and fellowship was lost. Paul told the Corinthians that those who felt others were unworthy to eat with them were themselves unworthy to be included in the Lord's Supper. The only reason one could even join in the Lord's Supper is because of the grace of God, and so excluding some of God's own children from the celebration of grace was rejecting the very concept of God's inclusion for anyone.

Deeming people unworthy doesn't always happen as dramatically as scripture describes. We almost unconsciously ostracize others for being irritating, uncool, or inconvenient. It might be easy to justify not hiring a refugee because they can't speak English, or someone in substance abuse treatment because they have a prison record. Sal and Cindy found their lives and their business rewarded for working to overcome barriers to employment such as language skills, or mistakes in their past. Sal worked with a hostess some felt was too forward—she had to be reprimanded for accepting gifts from customers and grabbing and holding people's babies, but she became a well-loved member of The Café community. Sal saw her as "a spreader of joy." If Sal and Cindy were concerned with strictly following rules, another employee, Christy Strauss, who became a manager at The Café, would never have been hired: her tattoos and piercings violated the employee manual. When that was pointed out to Sal, he conceded the handbook was "antiquated."

There are only two miracles recounted in all four Gospels. One, of course, is the resurrection of Jesus Christ. The other is the feeding of the multitudes (Matt 14:13–21, Mark 6:35–44, Luke 9:10–17, John 6:1–15). In that story, Jesus and his disciples are confronted with the overwhelming need of a crowd of people who had listened to Jesus all day. They were all hungry, and there was very little food. The disciples' solution was to send them all away. After all, they were unequipped to care for them all and it was each person's responsibility to find their own food. They

Mark 6:35-44

³⁵ Late in the day, his disciples came to him and said, "This is an isolated place, and it's already late in the day. ³⁶ Send them away so that they can go to the surrounding countryside and villages and buy something to eat for themselves."

³⁷ He replied, "You give them something to eat."

But they said to him, "Should we go off and buy bread worth almost eight months' pay and give it to them to eat?"

³⁸ He said to them, "How much bread do you have? Take a look."

After checking, they said, "Five loaves of bread and two fish."

³⁹ He directed the disciples to seat all the people in groups as though they were having a banquet on the green grass. ⁴⁰ They sat down in groups of hundreds and fifties. ⁴¹ He took the five loaves and the two fish, looked up to heaven, blessed them, broke the loaves into pieces, and gave them to his disciples to set before the people. He also divided the two fish among them all. ⁴² Everyone ate until they were full. ⁴³ They filled twelve baskets with the leftover pieces of bread and fish. ⁴⁴ About five thousand had eaten.

could feed their souls, but not their bodies. It was simply an impossible situation.

But Jesus turned to his disciples and said, "You feed them." Imagine their surprise and frustration. They had almost nothing! There they stood with not even enough to feed themselves, looking out over a sea of hungry faces. But Jesus commanded them to take what little they had and begin the work of distributing the food among the crowd. Obediently, they began, probably glancing at one another in alarm and nervous about what they would say to the next person when there was no more to give. But each time they reached into their baskets, there was more. They never ran out. It's easy to imagine Jesus smiling as their wonder grew. They were following the commands of Jesus and so Jesus provided.

Two things were needed for this miracle. The first thing that was needed was obedient servants. Jesus commanded his disciples to feed the people. They felt woefully inadequate. Anyone could see that they were being tasked with something that was completely impossible! But they stepped out in faith. They never stopped reaching into the basket, even when they were sure it must have been empty, because they were following the commands of their Lord.

The second, of course, was Christ himself. The love of Christ for his people was the power that enabled the food to keep multiplying, meeting their

Matthew 6:25-33

25 "Therefore, I say to you, don't worry about your life, what you'll eat or what you'll drink, or about your body, what you'll wear. Isn't life more than food and the body more than clothes? 26 Look at the birds in the sky. They don't sow seed or harvest grain or gather crops into barns. Yet your heavenly Father feeds them. Aren't you worth much more than they are? 27 Who among you by worrying can add a single moment to your life? 28 And why do you worry about clothes? Notice how the lilies in the field grow. They don't wear themselves out with work, and they don't spin cloth. 29 But I say to you that even Solomon in all of his splendor wasn't dressed like one of these. 30 If God dresses grass in the field so beautifully, even though it's alive today and tomorrow it's thrown into the furnace, won't God do much more for you, you people of weak faith? 31 Therefore, don't worry and say, 'What are we going to eat?' or 'What are we going to drink?' or 'What are we going to wear?' 32 Gentiles long for all these things. Your heavenly Father knows that you need them. 33 Instead, desire first and foremost God's kingdom and God's righteousness, and all these things will be given to you as well."

needs. This love is infused throughout the world, waiting for the broken and those in hardship to call on him. Christ is the source for our strength and our hope. Matthew 6:25–33 assures believers that God is aware of our needs and that we can trust in that care.

This does not mean that God's people will never be in want, because all of us deal with struggles in our lives. But what it does mean is that we can be confident of the love and care of the Lord, and through all of our difficulties, God will walk with us. Sometimes the basket will be full exactly as we wish. Sometimes we will be handed things we didn't expect. But through it all, Christ is there to be our guide and our salvation.

Imagine what must have been going through the heads of the people waiting on the hillside. They must have thought, just like the disciples, that the basket would be empty by the time their turn would come, too. But Jesus provided, just like he provided for Brandy Lee. She was a worker at The Café who once felt that addiction had taken away every chance for healing and redemption. When she arrived at The Café, she was sure that the basket would be empty by the time it got to her. But she was given a second chance by Sal and Cindy.

Brandy Lee's example highlights the communal nature of a full basket. Just as the crowd at the gathering with Jesus was required for the miracle to

John 21:15-17

¹⁵ When they finished eating, Jesus asked Simon Peter, "Simon son of John, do you love me more than these?"

Simon replied, "Yes, Lord, you know I love you."

Jesus said to him, "Feed my lambs." ¹⁶ Jesus asked a second time, "Simon son of John, do you love me?"

Simon replied, "Yes, Lord, you know I love you."

Jesus said to him, "Take care of my sheep." ¹⁷ He asked a third time, "Simon son of John, do you love me?"

Peter was sad that Jesus asked him a third time, "Do you love me?" He replied, "Lord, you know everything; you know I love you."

Jesus said to him, "Feed my sheep."

happen, Brandy Lee wasn't alone, and neither were Sal and Cindy. They were not experts in addiction treatment, so they partnered with an organization called Volunteers of America, with a track record of helping people to recovery. Thousands of others were involved as well—Brandy Lee stood with Sal and others as part of a Volunteers of America news conference, with TV cameras recording. The story of her success was a gospel that needed to be spread in order to help even more people.

Sal and Cindy were obedient to the command of Christ, and Jesus kept their basket full. There was enough to give Brandy a new life.

This is what we, as disciples, are called to do—to keep reaching into the basket in order to give the gift of God's love and grace to those around us. The Gospel of John ends with the resurrected Jesus sharing a meal on a beach with his disciples (John 21:15–17). They had been fishing unsuccessfully before he arrived, but when they followed his directions their nets overflowed with fish. As they grilled some of their bounty for breakfast, Jesus turned to Peter and asked if Peter loved him. Confused and a little shocked by the question, Peter assured him that he did. "Feed my lambs," Jesus answered. Three times Jesus initiated the same exchange. Three times Peter, hurt and confused, assured Jesus that he loved him. And three times, Jesus told him to "feed my lambs."

Like Peter, we may find following instructions to feed the lambs perplexing, and even as hard and as risky as wading into a crowd with presumably empty baskets. Sal and Cindy took a risk when Cindy promised employees she would cover for them in a family emergency. She took on the hard work of accompanying refugee families to school orientations, helping them get to courses that would help them pass their citizenship exam, and arranging for "English corners" to help families learn their new language. With one group of refugees Sal took a chance that was both in the self-interest of his business, but also reaching into the basket without being sure what the result would be. "I was only going to hire two of them," he said, adding, "then I said, 'We'll just hire all of them. We'll figure out where we're going to put them.'"

The work of discipleship is to love as Jesus loves, caring for others, both body and soul, with the abundance that God provides.

Questions:

1. Think of the times that you have bonded with other people over a meal. Why do you think that eating together forges such a strong connection with others?

2. Some of the members of the Corinthian church put their personal status and needs above that of

other members of their faith community. Do you see any examples of similar actions in today's faith communities? How is that an affront to grace?

3. As disciples of Jesus Christ, we are called to be Jesus's "basket carriers," even when the task seems impossible. When have there been times in your life where you have been obedient to Christ's call and been amazed by God's abundance?

4. Jesus told Peter to "feed my sheep." What did he mean? How do you respond to that command in your life?

Chapter 3:
When community calls
—listening to God

A church worker was talking to a homeless man on the streets of Washington, DC, when a stray dog ran into the road and was nearly hit by a car. Immediately the car stopped, and then another. People jumped out of their vehicles and coaxed the frightened dog to them, calming him before loading him up in one of their cars to take him to a safer place. The homeless man watched all of this in silence before turning to the church worker and stating, "I should have been born a dog."

How does the world value broken and struggling people? Our prisons are overflowing with them. Desperate migrants are turned away at borders and forced to live in camps in horrible conditions. Major cities all have homeless encampments. People stand on street corners by traffic lights asking for spare change to buy food. Yet every one of these people, despite their history or their circumstances, is beloved by God.

And because they are beloved by God, they are all people of great worth. Despite what we see when we look at them, God sees them as who they were created to be. God knows the special gifts he gave to each one of them. God knows what their struggles are and how they are trying to overcome them. God watches each one of them, his heart being broken by their failures and their suffering.

God doesn't sorrow only for those who we think of as struggling and broken, though. Every person on the planet has at one time or another broken God's heart because each of us is stained and soiled by sin. No one is who God created them to be. Every one of us was created in the image of God, but sin has distorted that image in all of us. The grace of God's remarkable love is that, despite that, the creator and sustainer of the cosmos loves each one of us and sees us for who we could be. God sees into our hearts and knows our yearnings to be whole and faultless. His desire is for each of us to see others in the same way: flawed by sin, but a holy creation waiting to be reborn. In John 15:12, Jesus said, "This is my commandment: love each other just as I have loved you." Jesus was asking that we see everyone through the same eyes of grace that we are blessed with when Christ looks at us.

That is what Sal and Cindy saw in Melinda Quire.

Cindy first spotted Melinda during a Christmas gathering at a halfway house. Melinda was a bewildered new arrival hoping to end years of drug addiction. What Cindy saw was a woman struggling in ways Cindy felt she had struggled as well. "I connected with her brokenness," Cindy said. Months later, when Melinda applied for a job with Sal, he didn't see a life of substance dependency and prison, but someone eager to accept even a job as a dishwasher. "I think that's a statement of character," said Sal.

Melinda quickly synced with Cindy's vision for the restaurant. She described her treatment at The Café by saying, "They didn't look at you like you had all those problems. They looked at what you could be, or what you were becoming."

In Philippians 2:3–5, Paul wrote, "Don't do anything for selfish purposes, but with humility think of others as better than yourselves. Instead of each person watching out for their own good, watch out for what is better for others. Adopt the attitude that was in Christ Jesus." Paul knew that pride and ego are fatal to the servant heart of a true disciple. The key is to see and respect the dignity of each human being, despite their background, history, or struggles. Jesus often sat and talked with those others thought were beneath him. He ate with tax collectors, prostitutes, and sinners, but he always saw each person through the eyes of love and valued them.

God has given every person the ability to enrich others somehow. Sometimes this ability is buried so deeply in sin and struggle that it's nearly impossible to see. Loving others as Jesus loves is risky and exposes vulnerability. Relationships fail and people get hurt. But disciples of Jesus Christ are called to take that risk. Sometimes it doesn't work. Sal often had to lay off employees who were not committed to their jobs. One of Sal's friends said, "Sal is not a pushover. He fires more people in a year than you or I would fire in a lifetime. But not randomly and not without a warning. He's a hard-nosed pragmatist at getting a day's work out of every person."

But sometimes taking the risk blesses us beyond measure. Hebrews 13:1–2 says, "Keep on loving each other as brothers. Do not forget to entertain strangers, for by so doing some people have entertained angels without knowing it."

This is the same attitude that Sal and Cindy tried to take. They asked about their employees' native countries. They were curious about their backgrounds and sincerely wanted to learn about them. They didn't see their employees as just a way to get work, but as human beings with hopes, dreams, and unique ways of looking at the world. They were people they could learn from. They built relationships with them as individuals.

Cindy's relationship with Marian, a refugee from Cuba who struggled with English, showed how trust rewarded risk, and what community can mean. Cindy trusted Marian with greater responsibility, and Marian responded. When Cindy saw Marian's concern about her son's health, she recommended a hospital. For another refugee employee, Cindy covered for her to take an extended vacation to see family in her homeland. Going those extra miles built relationships that not only respected employee dignity and humanity, but was returned with appreciation, dedication, and long-term employment—more than 15 years in Marian's case, unheard of in the restaurant business. While Sal and Cindy started just desperate to match a body to a job description, they discovered they had actually hired extraordinary people who helped grow the business. And it built lifelong personal friendships.

What Sal and Cindy did was to see and treat their employees as complete people, rather than as roles. One missionary said of Sal and Cindy, "They're in a relationship with their employees as individuals. When people can go to work in a place where not only are they not discriminated against, but they're loved, that's life-changing." Another missionary described

John 5:2-9

[2] In Jerusalem near the Sheep Gate in the north city wall is a pool with the Aramaic name Bethsaida. It had five covered porches, [3] and a crowd of people who were sick, blind, lame, and paralyzed sat there. [5] A certain man was there who had been sick for thirty-eight years. [6] When Jesus saw him lying there, knowing that he had already been there a long time, he asked him, "Do you want to get well?"

[7] The sick man answered him, "Sir, I don't have anyone who can put me in the water when it is stirred up. When I'm trying to get to it, someone else has gotten in ahead of me."

[8] Jesus said to him, "Get up! Pick up your mat and walk." [9] Immediately the man was well, and he picked up his mat and walked.

refugee families as "dying for inclusion…the thing refugees need the most, just being seen."

Don't we all?

How can we impact lives like that? Jesus was able to change lives and heal people with only touches and glances, but careful reading of scripture shows that that was not all he did. John 5:2–9 recounts a healing of an invalid who sat by a pool of water, probably Bethsaida in Jerusalem. Occasionally the pool would bubble up, and it was believed that the first person to enter the pool into the bubbles would be healed. But this man had sat by the pool for thirty-eight years, never able to get up quickly enough before someone beat him to it. His solution just wasn't working, but he sat there still.

The first thing Jesus did was actually see this man. Often that is the most profound thing we can do. How often do we walk past others, not even acknowledging their presence? Sometimes we honestly don't see them, and sometimes we don't want to take the responsibility that might come by seeing them. But Jesus saw this man, stopped, and initiated a conversation.

The next thing Jesus did was ask him a question. Jesus asked him if he wanted to get well. One would think that of course he would want to be well—who wouldn't? But Jesus took the time to listen and to truly learn this man's circumstances. He didn't rush in with solutions. He learned the man's situation and what he had been trying to do to solve it himself. He honored the man by respecting his story.

Notice the man didn't really answer Jesus's question. He gave reasons as to why he was still where he was. He had given up hope, but he was still trying ineffective solutions, still stuck in the same situation. He really couldn't see any other way. Jesus gave him a new solution. The man didn't need the pool at all. Jesus removed the barriers. All he had to do was to stand up and walk.

Perhaps Jesus had done the same for others, but they hadn't believed in Jesus or themselves enough to try to stand. Maybe they hadn't really wanted to be healed. The man had to stand up on his own, but Jesus had made it possible. The healing was a true relationship, initiated and enabled by Jesus, but ultimately enacted by the man.

Sal and Cindy offered second chances by seeing the whole person, but they didn't hand out second chances as a gift. They wanted something in return—they expected employees to perform, to stand up and walk on their own. Expecting people to take responsibility shows its own kind of compassion because it bestows dignity by allowing people to excel in their own way.

Sal and Cindy gave an especially profound explanation of how The Café helped people walk on their own. When they sold the restaurant and the new owners planned to start serving alcohol, some customers and employees wondered if it would still be a safe place for workers in treatment for substance abuse. Cindy explained that The Café never banned its employees from drinking—some still did go out after work. Instead, she said they offered an example that restaurant work didn't have to mean irresponsible partying. Sal said what The Café offered wasn't so much a restaurant without alcohol, but an attitude. He said, "We try to nip negativity in the bud when it occurs. We try to promote positivity." Sal and Cindy saw through society's stereotypes to the basis of a worker's outlook on life. From the hiring process through the daily workday, they nurtured what an employee could be.

All throughout scripture, Jesus honored those who had been rejected by society. He spoke with Samaritans, tax collectors, prostitutes, and thieves. He saw through their labels to the person beyond. Jesus gave them dignity, and with that dignity came hope for a new life as they grew into the person that God created them to be.

As Sal and Cindy met those who had been rejected by society, they responded in grace and love, too. Bringing them into their business looked risky, sometimes entailed lots of work, and could even look foolish to outsiders. But that's the very core of our faith. We are called to love one another because we are loved by God.

Questions:

1. Who are the people that society doesn't value? Why don't we value them?

2. How could it change relationships between people to remember that every person is beloved by God?

3. What risks do we take by trying to approach others with the mind of Christ? How can we balance those risks while being obedient to the call of loving others?

4. How can you relate the story of Jesus healing the invalid by the pool to your own interactions with other people? How did Jesus honor the man's dignity in the midst of help and healing?

5. It almost seems human nature, especially these days, to emphasize the negative, and even to hold on to negativity and act on it in daily life. What is a Christian view of negativity and positivity?

Chapter 4:
It's not "just business"
—the bottom-line case for faithful integrity

"It's just business."

What do people mean when they say that? Usually it means that they believe that ethics between friends are different than ethics at work. When people say "It's just business" they mean that, to them, the bottom line is more important than relationships, so people should not take business dealings personally. It's bad business to let relationships stand in the way of making money. To be successful, sometimes you have to be cold.

At least that's what we're told.

Cindy had exactly that experience in the restaurant business. "It was about the job and it was cutthroat when we learned the business—okay, if you don't do this, you don't have a job, you're outta here, we've got someone else who will take your place."

In places like that, workers are seen as a commodity. Sometimes promises are broken or the workplace becomes a toxic, angry place. Both employees and employers lose trust in one another and take advantage of each other. The "it's just business" attitude can also extend outside the company itself. Maybe the business is run on strictly what is legal but not always what is ethical. But looking back on their time in The Café, Cindy and Sal felt that running their business based on Christian ethics was a means to their success on every level: economic, spiritual, and personal. They would tell you that it is wrong to think that doing the right thing just *can* be good business. It *is* good business.

By not treating employees as commodities, Sal and Cindy learned that doing the right thing is good business. Too often employers see refugees and other nontraditional hires as sources of cheap labor. While The Café at first saw second-chance employees as a desperate way to find anyone to fill the slot, by seeing the whole person, Sal and Cindy discovered pools of talent that business owners seek but say are in short supply. The inherent traits these workers brought to the job included appreciation, dedication, creative problem-solving, autonomy, and longevity. But an even deeper and more valuable result of bonding with them was that the employees were able to see and act on the vision Sal and Cindy had for the business.

Sal and Cindy's hiring strategies combined good business strategies with compassion. But it can be difficult to know how to live out faith in a business setting because Christian behavior and smart business practices can sometimes seem in opposition. How can we balance our moral responsibilities with the often cutthroat business world?

The most reliable measure is to compare our own behavior with the character of God, questioning what God would have us do in each situation. It helps to weigh each decision by three divine characteristics that have direct bearing on ethics: faithful integrity, justice, and love.

Faithful integrity means that one's first allegiance is to God. Integrity is so often used as a synonym for honesty that it's helpful to go back to its broader definition of "soundness," "completeness," "being whole or undivided." Faithful integrity means God is likely not okay with the phrase, "It's just business."

Justice means respecting the dignity and rights of individuals and honoring commitments and promises. When everyone follows the rules that have been structured for both employers and employees, everyone knows what is expected and feels that they are being treated fairly. That's a very good thing that keeps a business running smoothly.

But we've all heard stories about times when the rules get in the way of compassion. Maybe an employee has a family emergency and doesn't come in for a shift when scheduled and then gets fired.

Perhaps a cashier comes up short once and then loses her job. The employer might be following the concept of justice by strictly following the rules, but Jesus taught that there are times that justice—following the established rules—must be tempered by love.

Justice and love are often in tension with one another—grace and forgiveness mean bending the rules for love. But bending the rules too many times for an employee might be unfair to the other workers who are having to work late to cover the missed shift or see a co-worker's hand in the till. Deciding when to practice justice and when to temper it with love takes prayer and deep thought. Important decisions are often not as easy and clear as wrong or right. Life is nuanced, and that calls for approaching it with love.

Love means dealing with your friends, neighbors, employees, and even with your enemies with grace, forgiveness, and compassion. It could mean giving them a break when maybe they don't deserve it. It could mean stepping back and putting yourself in their place to get some perspective on their situation. It probably means a bit of sacrifice on your part to enable another when they might need a helping hand. Jesus taught that love is treating someone as you would want to be treated yourself.

God doesn't condemn financial success, but that's not God's first priority in anyone's life. Allowing ambition to overshadow God's direction means that your work is no longer honoring God. Cindy and Sal, after prayer and deliberation, decided to close their restaurant on Sundays. They realized that God's teaching about a day of rest was directly applicable to their business, even though it was the most profitable day of the week.

The story of The Café closing on Sunday offers several lessons in the struggle between decency and profitability. For years Sal and Cindy fought what could be seen as clear messages telling them to honor the Sabbath. They regretted having to miss church. They recognized their employees would have valued the day off. Their son told them over and over they should close for a Sabbath to honor God and they would be richly rewarded. Even a Mother's Day meltdown of the kitchen and wait staff that had Cindy vowing "no more Mother's Days" wasn't enough to make them shut down their most profitable day of the week. Although a Sunday closing seemed unrealistic, Sal did hear the repeated messages about taking a Sabbath. He kept reworking his spreadsheets in search of a solution. So his mind and spirit were open when a friend suggested a practical, simple-seeming solution: open an hour earlier and close an hour later on other days.

As their son predicted, they were richly rewarded—in employee appreciation, but also in dollars and cents. The plan to replace Sunday service by extending hours the rest of the week quickly brought in more than the income they were making on Sunday. By closing the five hours they were open on Sunday and replacing those with opening two more hours the rest of the days, The Café was actually operating seven more hours a week. The after-church crowd grumbled a bit about losing a Sunday brunch option, then switched to brunching on Saturdays, further boosting revenue by turning that marginal day much busier.

Another case where the right answer was not obvious involved Jeff, an employee who relapsed several times and lied about it. It would have been easy to justify firing him. Instead, Sal took a chance by letting him come back, but only if he went into treatment. It was the first time Sal had tried anything like that. It was a journey through the differing demands created by faithful integrity, justice, and love.

"There's a fine line when you're trying to help people in recovery," said Sal. "You have to have compassion for them but also not enable them to pull the wool over your eyes." It takes prayer for God's guidance and courage to follow through on one's convictions.

Sal said his goal was to get Jeff back to work. The reason Sal made an exception for Jeff may go back to a human connection between the two. "I liked him as a person," said Sal, "and he's told me I was the closest thing he's had to a real dad. You can't have someone tell you that and it not make you feel warm and fuzzy."

Business-as-usual rules can provide excuses for not acting with both justice and love. An employer might be justified in not hiring a refugee—not being able to speak English could be a huge barrier to getting things done, maybe even dangerous where a quick warning about a hot stove could prevent an accident. Or someone with a prison record could be assumed to be dishonest. Looking beyond rigid codes to see who a person *could be* turned out to be Sal and Cindy's secret of success.

Ethical living is a delicate balance of all three characteristics: faithful integrity, justice, and love. While some argue that the Bible isn't relevant to today's complex business world, it's still the most profound and important guide we have to understand how to balance God's will with business. The book of Ephesians discusses Christian behavior in business as well as in community life. Specifically, Ephesians 4:25–32 examines how becoming a follower of Jesus Christ demands ethical conduct all the time.

Ethical conduct all the time begins with truthfulness. Truthfulness goes beyond just "not lying" because it also prohibits fostering false assumptions. People have to be able to trust one another. It's impossible to work together towards a common goal without trust. The writer of Ephesians compared

Ephesians 4:25-32

²⁵ Therefore, after you have gotten rid of lying, Each of you must tell the truth to your neighbor because we are parts of each other in the same body. ²⁶ Be angry without sinning. Don't let the sun set on your anger. ²⁷ Don't provide an opportunity for the devil. ²⁸ Thieves should no longer steal. Instead, they should go to work, using their hands to do good so that they will have something to share with whoever is in need.

²⁹ Don't let any foul words come out of your mouth. Only say what is helpful when it is needed for building up the community so that it benefits those who hear what you say. ³⁰ Don't make the Holy Spirit of God unhappy—you were sealed by him for the day of redemption. ³¹ Put aside all bitterness, losing your temper, anger, shouting, and slander, along with every other evil. ³² Be kind, compassionate, and forgiving to each other, in the same way God forgave you in Christ.

working together in truth to being parts of the same body. Anything that damages one damages all.

Truthfulness and trust don't mean that things always work out. Sal often had to lay off workers who didn't hold up their end. But truthfulness means being open and honest and forthcoming when there are problems, and treating each person with integrity.

Growing up, Sal caddied for his dad, whose friends would pull Sal aside and remark how different Sal's dad was. He wouldn't participate in their bawdy banter—a trait that earned him respect. As Sal rode with his father, helping out on air conditioning repair trips, his father would stress to Sal the importance of honest service—he wouldn't recharge the freon without first checking for a leak. Sal's dad saw that as a competitive business edge. It would take Sal decades to learn those lessons, but he first heard from his father about faithful integrity, and about how doing the right thing is good business.

In any situation where people work together, eventually something will happen to cause anger. The passage in Ephesians 4:26–27 is pragmatic about this. It doesn't condemn being angry, but it warns against letting anger take over and be in control. Anger is not an excuse for sin. The writer of Ephesians also knew that anger can irritate and build up resentment. The writer counseled dealing with the situation right away and "not letting the sun go down on your anger." Allowing those emotions to fester only causes them to grow, causing embitterment and poisoning relationships.

Sal's anger and resentment over Jeff in particular could have cost a valued worker, and even a life. As a result of Jeff's relapses and lying about reasons for missing work, Sal felt betrayed. Mistreated. Angry. It was Cindy who pointed out that if Jeff didn't get help, he'd likely die.

Sal stepped out of the normal boss-worker relationship and took Jeff to rehab. Once there he was supposed to be left alone, to cure himself. But one evening they broke another rule. "It's Christmas," Sal said to Cindy. "We've got to do something for this guy." They took Jeff a pair of slippers.

Jeff would return to The Café, get more responsibility, fall in love, and adopt a daughter. "I get to wake up and see a smile," Jeff would say. "It's the little things in life that I missed so much of for so many years."

Related to honesty is theft. It isn't uncommon for workers to engage in petty theft, but not paying a fair wage, expecting workers to stay after hours without pay, or making them cover work expenses out of their own pocket is theft as well. Both theft by employees and theft by employers are demoralizing and destroy the cohesion of a healthy work environment.

Scripture also admonishes against harsh or demeaning speech. Sal got taught that lesson by a Muslim refugee. As he stormed around the kitchen, taking inventory, moving containers around and swearing up a storm, she stopped him. Don't curse, she lectured. "Say 'Thank you, God, I woke up today.'" Now Sal says, "We discourage the use of foul language. Cindy and I have worked in restaurants with a culture of thinking the way you get things done is by being mean and pushy. But it's not necessary. You can actually run a kitchen without dropping the f-bomb every other word."

Ephesians 5:4 tells us, "Obscene language, silly talk, or vulgar jokes aren't acceptable for believers. Instead, there should be thanksgiving." Words should build up, not tear down. Sometimes in the workplace, people speak rudely or roughly in order to fit in, but Ephesians says that if what you say doesn't benefit another, don't say it. Sal's explanation for avoiding foul language makes the point that crudity is more than just words, but an attitude toward people and life. Ephesians 4:29 teaches that it's not just avoiding negativity, but reaching for positivity: "Don't let any foul words come out of your mouth. Only say what is helpful when it is needed for building up the community so that it benefits those who hear what you say."

Ephesians ends its instruction by listing everything that is detrimental to the right workings of a community: bitterness, losing one's temper, anger, shouting, and slander. Instead, the passage says that one should "live your life with love, following the example of Christ," being loving, kind, compassionate, and forgiving.

In any work situation, a Christian should never lose sight of the value of any person that they are dealing with, be it employee, customer, or employer. Persons, even the rude, lazy, or undependable ones, are beloved children of God. That doesn't mean that every person is a good employee and should always stay in a job, but every person does deserve honesty and to have their dignity preserved.

Sal once faced down a staff conflict in a way that showed how a dispassionate, hard-nosed approach that focused on business goals blends with compassion and maintaining dignity. Responding to server complaints that the hostess wasn't being fair to the wait staff when seating customers, Sal gathered all the workers and played the Carole King song "Beautiful" that includes the lyric, "You've got to get up every morning/With a smile on your face/And show the world all the love in your heart." Sal showed a spreadsheet indicating that tables were actually being distributed fairly, and the servers and the hostess had a chance to comment. Sal emphasized that no customer should ever see a hostess calculating how to seat them based on employee needs. The meeting ended with everyone agreeing to work together. Eventually, one of the servers who had complained found another job and left The Café.

"Sometimes it's just not fixable," says Sal, or, more precisely, "I don't want them to think all they've got to do is come and tell me and I'm going to wave a magic wand and it's all going to go away....I can be the catalyst or the coach...but it's not about me fixing it. It's about us working together to resolve these issues." Sal needed a smooth-running dining room. Rather than scolding or accusing, he honestly and clearly described that goal, allowing employees the dignity of choosing how to react, even if it meant them (eventually) deciding (on their own) to leave.

Once when Sal was looking for new hires, he was approached by Ron McKiernan, who was a rehabilitation counselor and a recovering alcoholic himself. Ron had changed his own life and then worked to change others' lives, starting with intervention sessions for substance abusers, then detox, and finally placing them in jobs so that they had a new framework for their lives that focused on sobriety. Ron asked Sal to hire some of the people he had been counseling.

Sal wasn't crazy about the idea, but he had an opening for a dishwasher, a back-of-the-kitchen position that didn't interact with customers. The work was hard and exhausting, and he had had trouble keeping it filled. Ron sent Casey Wagner, who opened Sal's eyes to understanding the value of a second chance. What struck Sal about Casey was that he did not look like the stereotypical drug abuser—he was a clean-cut kid from a prominent family and a good school, who also happened to be about the same age as Sal's son. Casey did well as an employee—so well he eventually left The Café to earn an MBA, get progressively more impressive jobs, marry, and raise a family. Casey's model behavior as a treatment program success helped Sal learn about working with future second-chance employees who weren't always so perfect.

Adopting Christian ethics in the business world means a re-evaluation of goals. Instead of money-making and self-promotion, focus shifts to honoring God through vocations and work. After Sal and Cindy sold their business, they were able to look back with contentment and pride in what they had accomplished.

"You can have a good outcome and not feel like you're the person you don't want to be," Cindy said. "We did something good in the industry."

Questions

1. How do people sometimes view ethics in business as different from ethics in everyday living? What does that say about relationships inside and outside of the business world?

2. What tension do you see between the three characteristics of divine ethics (faithful integrity, justice, and love)? Can you be true to all three all the time?

3. Cursing and obscenity have become a lot more common in popular culture. Is this just an expressive use of words or a trend that conflicts with faith principles? What should we do, or not do, about it?

4. "Every person, even a rude, lazy, or undependable one, is a beloved child of God." Do you agree with this statement? Would believing this statement change your behavior? How?

5. Sal's attitudes and reactions to people in substance abuse recovery changed after meeting someone who didn't fit his image of a drug abuser. How can we do a better job of looking beyond stereotypes and stigmas and into each individual's value as a person?

6. Do you feel as though your current business practices honor God? Would you change them? How?

Chapter 5:
When the going gets tough
—going through life instead of around it

G.K. Chesterton, a British writer and theologian, wrote, "Christianity has not been so much tried and found wanting, as it has been found difficult and left untried."

Sadly, that is often the reason people abandon their faith at the office door. It's not that they don't respect Christian ethics, but they feel it's just too hard to apply them in a dog-eat-dog business environment. A notable example of this double standard is John D. Rockefeller. Considered to be the richest man in the modern era, he was so ruthless in business that anti-trust and monopoly laws are based on preventing any other company ever using his business tactics again. Although most of what he did was legal at the time, there is little argument that it was unethical. The *New York World* wrote that Rockefeller's Standard Oil was "the most cruel, impudent, pitiless, and grasping monopoly that ever fastened upon a country." However, Rockefeller was also deeply religious and, in later life, became one of the greatest philanthropists in history, founding educational institutions and supporting medical research. He considered himself a devout Christian and said that his faith was the guiding force in his life and the reason for his success.

Rockefeller honored God in his private life, but he didn't allow God to rule over his business decisions. Instead of being fully obedient to God, he only allowed God access over part of his life. Clearly, that's not what Jesus taught. But if a person rejects the idea of dual morality—that ethics are different in the business world—how do they go about living out Christian values in an often cutthroat, secular world?

One place to start is to examine your own goals. Sal and Cindy once had a goal of running a successful chain of seafood restaurants. That goal was in almost direct conflict with their college dreams of creating a cozy little café where, Cindy would later say, "I would run it fair and honest and treat people with dignity."

With the seafood restaurant, they went big. And they cut corners. The concept was to offer low prices and extremely high volume, with an overall strategy of expanding big enough to provide them a large income. They copied a restaurant in Florida, even to the ethically dubious point of sending their chef to apply for a job there so he could work just long enough to learn (well, actually, steal) their recipes. They even copied a version of the name until they received a cease-and-desist letter. When business shrank and they had to close one of the locations, they didn't choose the least-profitable building. Instead, they shuttered the one with a contract that allowed them to just lock the doors and walk away, even though business was better there. And when they closed it they did just lock the doors and walk away, surprising and angering the original investor and ruining what had been a strong professional relationship. It all spiraled downward still further and even threatened their marriage.

Their goals were wealth, status, personal self-fulfillment, and material goods. It was only when they shifted their goals and realigned them with their faith that they found a way forward.

When they re-created their business, they began looking at their restaurant as a way to honor and serve God. They realized that you don't need to be in ministry to honor God in your work. Every job, with the exception of immoral or unethical work, can be a way to bring God glory.

Most people in the Bible had jobs that were considered secular. Paul was a tentmaker. Peter was a fisherman. Even Jesus was a carpenter. But none of them made financial success their primary goal. Instead, their vocations were one of the ways in which they demonstrated their obedience and service to God. Their work was integrated into their lives, and their lives reflected their faith. Spiritual values became their core and so spiritual values drove their business decisions.

Those values can show up in management decisions, employee hiring, and even day-to-day attitudes. Victoria Petersen was a hostess at The Café who spread her love of life beyond her job title. She openly delighted in the customers, gushing over an unusual hat, or a baby. Her personality was especially notable, given a background of addiction and an eating disorder that eventually killed her. Even a scar on her forehead turned into an asset, with Sal complimenting the hats she wore to cover up the injury. That was all the encouragement she needed to turn the hats into a trademark for Victoria and The Café. She used her drug treatment as a lesson to a group of schoolchildren she talked to, popping out her false teeth for them to vividly illustrate one result of meth addiction. A woman who took Victoria under her wing to the point where Victoria called her "Mama" described the talents Victoria brought to the job, concluding, "People came to The Café to see Victoria. She lit up the room."

Describing another effect of Victoria's life, her adopted "mama" said, "She gave me the gift of having the best mother-daughter relationship for three and a half years that anyone could ever have.… Victoria's story is about a human being who had a rough start

Luke 12:13–21

¹³ Someone from the crowd said to him, "Teacher, tell my brother to divide the inheritance with me."

¹⁴ Jesus said to him, "Man, who appointed me as judge or referee between you and your brother?"

¹⁵ Then Jesus said to them, "Watch out! Guard yourself against all kinds of greed. After all, one's life isn't determined by one's possessions, even when someone is very wealthy." ¹⁶ Then he told them a parable: "A certain rich man's land produced a bountiful crop. ¹⁷ He said to himself, What will I do? I have no place to store my harvest! ¹⁸ Then he thought, Here's what I'll do. I'll tear down my barns and build bigger ones. That's where I'll store all my grain and goods. ¹⁹ I'll say to myself, You have stored up plenty of goods, enough for several years. Take it easy! Eat, drink, and enjoy yourself. ²⁰ But God said to him, 'Fool, tonight you will die. Now who will get the things you have prepared for yourself?' ²¹ This is the way it will be for those who hoard things for themselves and aren't rich toward God."

and had to learn how to love pretty much on her own and did it masterfully."

Time and time again, Jesus preached on focusing on "the greater thing," which was the rewards of a life of faith and righteousness. However, too many Christians seem to feel that money and possessions will come to them if they're just faithful. In a 2016 poll by Ligonier Ministries, 25% of American Christians agreed that "God will always reward true faith with material blessings." But that's not what scripture tells us. Luke 12:13–15 tells of a man who asked Jesus to arbitrate in an inheritance dispute. Jesus refused, warning the man, "Watch out! Guard yourself against all kinds of greed. After all, one's life isn't determined by one's possessions, even when someone is very wealthy." Jesus then told the crowd a parable about a rich man who stored up all his goods, but then died later that night. He had devoted his life to amassing possessions and they were all left behind, no longer his. The only thing that was truly important in his life was how he had responded to the call of the Lord, and in that, he was a failure. He died a very poor man indeed.

There are times that following spiritual values negatively impacts the bottom line. But that can depend on how you define the bottom line.

When Sal and Cindy decided to forego the traditional restaurant profit centers of serving alcohol and dinner, their goal was to save their marriage. Hiring workers from treatment programs was far in the future. They actually swore off restaurant work entirely, blaming it as an inherently family-unfriendly industry with long, late hours and a partying atmosphere.

When financial desperation and a restaurant business opportunity landed in their laps, they would only pursue it on their terms, with family as a priority. There would be no alcohol served. Not serving dinner was an easier decision—their restaurant was located in an antique mall that was only open from 10:00 a.m. till 6:00 p.m. And Sal and Cindy wouldn't even have a key to the place, so they couldn't arrive early or leave late.

Other life events further seemed to be telling them to change their priorities. A home kitchen accident that burned their son moved them to slow down and pay more attention to family. Involvement in their church opened their eyes to ways of welcoming people without judging them.

When Sal and Cindy closed their restaurant on the most profitable day of the week, Sunday, they did it in order to give their workers and themselves a day of rest. They paid attention to and acted on the human needs of their employees, even providing English lessons for some of their immigrant workers. Cindy attended school conferences with her employees so that they could have an advocate who would help them understand how to navigate their new lives. Their son described how The Café's after-closing English lessons would occasionally get interrupted by the demands of the end of the school day: "Sometimes my mom would be the one shuttling people back and forth, especially on snowy days when the weather was bad. She didn't want their kids standing at the city bus stop, so she would drive them home."

Sal and Cindy put people before profit, building a place of nurturing and support for people who were struggling to build new beginnings. It was an exhausting, demanding way of life for them. Not only did they have to run a business, they immersed themselves into other peoples' often messy and difficult lives. But living as a disciple of Jesus Christ is very often messy and difficult. Jesus rarely asks us to do things the easy way.

Sal and Cindy found themselves enriched and deepened by inviting messy lives into their own. Victoria, the hostess with the hats, had a difficult early family, drifted into drug abuse, worked as a table dancer, and moved from place to place as people would take her in. Sal wouldn't hire her at first because "she looked like a street person." Melinda Quire, a woman Cindy first spotted at a Christmas party at a halfway house, spent more than half her life in some kind of addiction before becoming an example for Cindy of someone who can turn their life around.

Casey Wagner, the second person Sal hired from a drug treatment program, changed Sal's views of addiction and played a key part in building The Café's compassionate business model.

It would have been tidier to hire from more traditional resumés, but choosing to live a life that puts honoring God first can be choosing the hard way.

Sal had an epiphany about trying to take the easy way out while hiking with his son. After they climbed a mountain together, he became frightened about climbing back down the rock face and insisted there must be another, easier way back down again.

It was supposed to be the perfect father-son bonding trip. Sal's son, Clark, had even climbed North Carolina's Cedar Rock himself a few weeks earlier, with some outdoor specialists. But Sal thought he knew better. Worried about the descent, he set out to find an easier path. No, Clark would say, all the expert advice is that there's only one way up and one way down. Sal thought he found another path but it ended in impassable thickets. Three times he tried. By then they'd missed the spectacular sunset they'd hiked up to see, and they hadn't even packed flashlights. Finally, Clark was able to guide them safely down, but as Sal was driving back home, he pulled over and broke into tears. Suddenly the literal trip to the mountaintop was a metaphor for his life—of looking for the easy way, of not listening, of figuratively hoping to win the lottery, of going around life rather than facing up and working through it. In opening the first overly ambitious restaurant, he listened to the voice seeking fortune and glory rather than to his heart. He asked Cindy for a divorce rather than facing the work of saving his family.

Up on that mountain, Sal learned humility. He learned that he didn't always know the better way, but that there were others he could depend on: his son, his wife, and especially God. Sal said that it was his "aha" moment when he realized that "I'm weak and I'm flawed." Facing—and accepting—our limitations allows us to accept help from others, building relationships that strengthen all involved. And listening to God, and accepting and obeying God's word, enabled Sal to "get in and dig it out" and find the strength to do the difficult things that doing things the right way often demands.

It is also scary. It's hard to challenge oneself to do the difficult thing, and it takes courage to face flaws, accept limitations, but go ahead anyway. Simply put, righteousness isn't for wimps.

Every one of us is limited, flawed, and, quite honestly, not up to the task of living a life that fully honors God. We are all often tempted to lie, to follow the letter of the law rather than the spirit of the law, to exploit people and situations, and to place more importance on personal material success than on honoring God. But the wonderful thing is that we have a God who knows us and loves us. God offers us grace and forgiveness, and, by facing our shortcomings with humility, we can pray to find the empathy to deal in grace with others.

Questions

1. In Matthew 19:24, Jesus told his disciples that "it's easier for a camel to squeeze through the eye of a needle than for a rich person to enter God's kingdom." Do you think Rockefeller would have agreed with that? What do you think Jesus would have said to Rockefeller?

2. What do you think about the poll that asked if God always rewarded faithfulness with material goods? Do you agree?

3. What are some of the "messy" ways that God has asked you to honor him?

4. What are some of your limitations you've discovered and how has God helped you to overcome them?

Isaiah 43:5-7

⁵ Don't fear,
 I am with you.
From the east I'll bring your children;
 from the west I'll gather you.
⁶ I'll say to the north, "Give them back!"
 and to the south, "Don't detain them."
Bring my sons from far away,
 and my daughters from the end of the earth,
 ⁷ everyone who is called by my name
 and whom I created for my glory,
 whom I have formed and made.

Chapter 6:
Bringing yourself to the table
—Christian accountability in the workplace

Why did God create us? Many theologians turn to Isaiah 43:7 to answer that question. There it says that God created us for his glory. Everyone who is "formed and made" is here on earth to glorify God.

But what does that mean?

If I sing hymns in church or shout out "Praise God!" when something good happens, am I fulfilling my purpose on earth by glorifying God? To a small extent, yes, but as discussed in the first chapter, honoring and glorifying God means that we act justly, love mercy, and walk humbly with our God (Micah 6:8). By living out our faith in obedience as visible disciples, we are glorifying the Lord through our own unique service to him. But God didn't leave us unequipped to do this. Each one of us was created with our own talents and abilities to add our praise to the Lord. Every one of us was created to honor God in our own distinct way.

Exodus 35:30-35

³⁰ Then Moses said to the Israelites: "Look, the Lord has chosen Bezalel, Uri's son and Hur's grandson from the tribe of Judah. ³¹ The Lord has filled him with the divine spirit that will give him skill, ability, and knowledge for every kind of work. ³² He will be able to create designs, do metalwork in gold, silver, and copper, ³³ cut stones for setting, carve wood, do every kind of creative work, ³⁴ and have the ability to teach others. Both he and Oholiab, Ahisamach's son from the tribe of Dan, ³⁵ have been given the skill to do every kind of work done by a gem cutter or a designer or a needleworker in blue, purple, and deep red yarns and in fine linen or a weaver or anyone else doing work or creating designs."

One of the best examples of this in the Bible is the construction of the tabernacle in Exodus. A large and very detailed section of Exodus outlines God's directions for building the tabernacle. Specific measurements, instructions for colors and decorations, and even recipes for the holy oils are described exactly. All of the Hebrew people were invited to join in the construction, each according to their own abilities. Those who were skilled in crafts, woodworking, weaving, embroidery, and metalwork were praised in the text, and it is the only place in the Bible where craftspeople were specifically mentioned by name and esteemed for their work (Exodus 35:30–35). Those who were not craftspeople brought freewill offerings of all the needed materials that they had collected, mined, or harvested, including gold and silver, wood, gemstones, wool, spices, and oil. Everyone had a means to join in the glorification of God.

And so it is today. Cindy, a skilled chef, used her talents in the kitchen to the glory of God. Sal used his abilities at business and marketing to help build a place of new beginnings for struggling people, glorifying God in the process. Those who worked in The Café demonstrated the power of God's grace and healing as they conquered the demons of poverty and addiction. As strange as it might seem, a little café by the railroad tracks in Louisville, Kentucky, glorified God each day it swung open its doors.

Maybe it is fitting. It was over a meal, in the Gospel of John, chapter 21, that Jesus gave his disciples his final commandment, to "feed my sheep." While Christ was always concerned about his followers' physical needs, even more important was how they could be satisfied spiritually. The little café in Louisville filled many bellies, but it filled hearts and souls as well. While Sal and Cindy didn't aggressively advertise their Christianity, when asked they were never shy about speaking about their faith. Mainly, it was their lived obedience to the call of Christ that was more powerful than anything they could say. Both customers and employees could see faith in action, expressed through their strength and compassion. They helped to make disciples of others by first being disciples themselves. By using the talents that God blessed them with to demonstrate a life that was more precious than silver or gold, they were able to bring others to that life as well.

Sal and Cindy glorified God not by preaching with words but with actions. They literally fed Jesus's sheep. They didn't quote Bible verses. Sal himself said he "struggles with evangelism." Food and customer service felt more natural to them than sermonizing. He said, "We try to find God where we are and not try to construct a temple for him. We're just trying to do our work and doing it in a way that honors him, not through pontificating or Bible thumping, but by being genuine Christians and trying to walk the walk." It's an approach endorsed by their minister, who said, "There is a call for us to make disciples, but you and I never win the first person to Christ. God's the one who does the work. Ours is to live a Christlike life.... The lesson is to make decisions based upon your faith, your core values.... The lesson is don't be afraid to be in a relationship with people."

Because each one of us is born with unique, God-given skills, we are expected to use them. Jesus told a parable in Matthew 25:14–30 about using talents for God. A talent was a mind-boggling sum of money in Jesus's time, equal to about fifteen years of work for a day laborer. It was because of this story that the word "talent" entered the language in the Middle Ages to describe a special ability given by God. In the story, a king gave one servant five talents, one two, and the last one talent to invest and grow for the king. The first two servants doubled their money, but the last only hid the talent in the ground to protect it. The last one squandered his opportunity to use the talent in service of the king, in effect wasting his life and not fulfilling his purpose on earth.

A modern-day church once asked for three volunteers to live out the story of the talents. One person received $50, one $20, and the last $10, and a year later they were asked to report back to the church to see what they had done with the money.

One man, a woodworker, spent the money on wood, built a beautiful desk, and sold it for three times his cost. One woman sewed a dress on commission and tripled her money, too. But the woman who was given the $10 bought baking supplies and started making baked goods for soldiers at the nearby military base. She reinvested the money she earned and kept baking throughout the year. By the end of the year, she had made several thousand dollars and had a thriving business that she continued, donating all that she earned to the church. While the others were successful in their mission, the last woman was persistent in using both the money given to her and her own talents to glorify God.

The parable of the talents was part of a series of stories that Jesus told about preparing oneself for judgment. The caution throughout all the stories was to realize that we don't always know how much time we have to glorify the Lord in our lives, and that there will be a final time of accountability before God. We were given the gifts of our time on earth, our abilities, and our talents to use in the service of discipleship, and God is concerned with how we are investing those things for the furtherance of the kingdom. It's important to realize that neither the master who distributed the talents nor the pastor of that modern-day church gave instructions to the recipients. Faithfulness is not just following directions.

It's active responsibility that takes initiative, risk, persistence, and creative thought.

Sal and Cindy used all those actions to create The Café, even though for much of their lives they felt more like they were just trying to hang on rather than glorifying God.

They took the initiative to go to a college that would prepare them for a career. They accepted entry-level jobs. They sought greater responsibility, rose in the ranks, opened their own restaurants. They risked money, laid their reputations on the line, even gambled hugely on buying a building so run-down Cindy cried when she first saw it. They dug deep into their creative thinking abilities, using them to solve problems, even spending years trying to figure out how they could close on Sunday without hurting the business. And if there's any one trait that most shines through in their story, it's persistence. They pushed through threats to their marriage, household financial strains, and a shattered family after Sal quit their first restaurant, leaving Cindy and her dad to pick up the pieces. When they finally opened their own building, they persevered through tax problems, power outages, an ice storm, and even a flood. "We were like, smitten," Sal half-joked.

While we often think about business skills and discipleship skills as being very different, initiative, risk, persistence, and creative thought are attributes of both of them. Sal and Cindy didn't just practice these attributes themselves, but strove to help others reach their own potentials by coaching and demonstrating them to their employees. They took risks with not only their time and money, but with people. They were persistent when people initially disappointed them. They thought creatively about what each person could bring to their jobs.

When Sal and Cindy, desperate for good workers, started their second-chance hiring, they entered worlds they knew almost nothing about, so they got help from people who did have the experience and expertise. They formed relationships with refugee and recovery organizations and learned from them not just how to survive, but thrive.

It's a difficult path to live as a disciple. Sal would meet weekly for breakfast with other Christians to discuss problems, try to guide one another in Christian practices, and, most importantly, provide accountability in their businesses. Cindy actually took a major business decision to a Christian retreat seeking an answer, then acted on that answer. They listened to their son, who urged them to honor God by closing on Sunday, mixing into that decision their own practical talents in what their minister called "a period of discernment."

For Cindy, Christian accountability had direct lessons for how to treat people in the workplace: "It's not about judging people on where they are in their world as far as their accomplishments, but appreciating someone just for who they are. Not for what they bring to the table."

Seeing the human being beyond the resumé offers a radical rethinking of the conventional wisdom of how to approach business. It formed the core of Sal and Cindy's success. A drug treatment program The Café had partnered with used another unusual hiring technique when it assigned jobs to those in the program. Instead of seeking the most qualified for the jobs running the center, people in the program would vote on candidates based on how the job would benefit them. Someone making fun of people cleaning toilets might find themself on the maintenance crew. Staying accountable to your Christianity can call for new approaches to "that's the way we've always done it."

Accountability is hardly a new concept, though. The apostle Peter challenged his own churches to be accountable to one another in both their daily practices and in using the gifts and abilities that God had given them. In 1 Peter 4:10–11, he wrote, "And serve each other according to the gifts each person has received, as good managers of God's diverse gifts. Whoever speaks should do so as those who speak God's word. Whoever serves should do so from the strength that God furnishes. Do this so that in everything God may be honored through Jesus Christ. To him be honor and power forever and always. Amen."

The word Peter used, translated here as "manager" was the Greek word *oikonomos*, usually meaning a slave who was entrusted with his master's property. Just as in the parable of the talents, we are entrusted with great gifts from the Lord, not the least of which is that of life itself.

May we use those gifts wisely, and give God honor through our discipleship to him.

Questions:

1. What are your unique talents and abilities that God has given you? Do you think that you are using them for God's glory?

2. What do you think of the small church's challenge of the talents? Do you think your church or faith group would benefit from a similar challenge?

3. Society often talks about a dichotomy between good discipleship and good business practices. Were you struck by reading that a good and faithful disciple will also employ practices that are necessary in business to succeed?

4. Why is accountability to other Christians important in discipleship?

5. Cindy's statement of not judging people for what they bring to the table but for who they are could seem difficult to achieve in the real world. How does an employer look past a resumé and see someone's potential? How did The Café make that work? How might that apply to your life?

About the authors

Sue Mink

After graduating with a degree in Graphic Design and working in an ad agency, Sue Mink wrote hand-knitting patterns, went to seminary, taught in an alternative high school, and is now writing theological studies, primarily for Abingdon Press, the publishing house of the United Methodist Church. She and her husband have two grown children. Since 2015, they live in a small town in Virginia during the summers and winters. In the spring and fall, they choose another place in the world to live for three months and work remotely. Some of the places they've chosen to live are Florence, Italy; Krakow, Poland; Taipei, Taiwan; and Bucharest, Romania.

Paul Wesslund

Paul Wesslund grew up in St. Paul, Minnesota, where he went to Macalester College. He worked four years as a reporter and copyeditor at daily newspapers in North Dakota, then moved to Washington, DC, to work at the National Rural Electric Cooperative Association as an energy writer and managing communications and community involvement programs. He worked the next twenty years as editor of *Kentucky Living* magazine and vice president for communications for the Kentucky Association of Electric Cooperatives in Louisville, before retiring to do freelance writing and communications consulting, including writing the book *Small Business, Big Heart: How One Family Redefined the Bottom Line.*

Paul is active in his church, St. Paul United Methodist in Louisville, where he helped start the Christian Action group that focuses on environmental and racial justice and church LGBTQ+ issues.

He and his wife, Debbie, live in Louisville, Kentucky, and have a daughter, Emma, who works in the Washington, DC, area, where she is involved in local theater. When Paul's not writing, he's likely attending a concert or curating his collection of music that includes jazz, classical, alternative and classic rock, country, electronic, African Soukous, and especially the blues.

Also by Paul Wesslund

www.ingramcontent.com/pod-product-compliance
Lightning Source LLC
Chambersburg PA
CBHW031456040426
42444CB00007B/1119